THE

FIRE ON THE HEARTH

IN

SLEEPY HOLLOW

A Christmas Poem of the Olden Time.

BY EDWARD HOPPER.

NEW YORK:
PUBLISHED BY HURD AND HOUGHTON,
401 *BROADWAY, COR. WALKER ST.*
1865.

RIVERSIDE, CAMBRIDGE:
STEREOTYPED AND PRINTED BY
H. O. HOUGHTON AND COMPANY

To

JOHN TAYLOR JOHNSTON, Esq.,

MY CLASSMATE AND LONG-TRIED, CONSTANT FRIEND,

This Poem

IS MOST RESPECTFULLY AND AFFECTIONATELY
DEDICATED.

THE FIRE ON THE HEARTH.

OH, the old-timed crackling fire
Upon the cheerful hearth!
Oh, the longing and desire
For the fire on the hearth!

In the blessed olden time
The open fireplace
Gave to our rugged clime
A cheery, rugged race.

Then home was bright and clear
When winter ruled the night;
Though storms blew loud and drear,
The house was warm and bright.

Around the glowing hearth
Gathered the old and young;
Brimful their hearts of mirth,
And pure the songs they sung.

When Christmas, old and bright,
Sent Santa Claus around
From house to house at night,
The stockings could be found.

He found the hearth full wide
For sledge and tiny deer,
And his good self beside,
Though big with Christmas gear.

Now furnace-holes and paint,
And hideous stove-pipes drear,
Shut out the dear old Saint
And half the Christmas cheer.

Our wise progressive race
By modern homestead laws
Have closed the fireplace
And banished Santa Claus.

Oh, the old-timed crackling fire
Upon the cheerful hearth!
Oh, the longing and desire
For the fire on the hearth!

WINTER EVENING.

When evening came of wintry day
  We turned from labor or from mirth,
With feet half frozen on our way,
  Crunching the snow upon the earth,
Bound homeward through the biting air;
  When first in sight of home we came,
Oh, how the brightening, crimson glare
  Of glowing coals and sparkling flame
Came rushing with bright smiles to meet us,
Came stretching forth warm hands to greet us,
Far through the evening's dusky shadows,
Now leaping over frozen meadows,
Climbing the hills with ruddy faces,
To give and to receive embraces, —
To bid us welcome home again!
So in Chaldea bright stars of even
Came down of old from seats in heaven
To whisper in the ears of men
The secrets of the worlds of light,
To cheer lone watchers of the night.

But we have quenched the cheery ray
  Which melts the heart of Winter cold,
And comfort changed for fashion's sway,
  And exiled the sweet home of old.

For now we keep the fire in prisons,
In iron dungeons low and dark;
The glare of gilt and paint bedizens,
But not one glimmer, not a spark
Of our old happy fire dare come
To rollick in our polished home.

THE HEARTH-STONE BANISHED.

We 've exiled old, red-headed Nestor,
The hearth-stone we 've turned out of door,
Our fire 's a heated "Nor'wester,"
Our hearth is a hole in the floor.

The youngsters, like prisoners breaking
From dungeon-walls, leave the dull place,
And the loves of the homestead forsaking,
Run down to perdition apace.

Fond husbands, the wretches, are ready
At evening to sup and be off,
With billiards and clubs grow unsteady,
And suitable subjects for Gough.

Some stick to the varnish and starching,
The polish and tinsel and glass,
But wearily sigh to be marching
With Nebuchadnezzar to grass.

HOMESTEAD ANGELS.

THE home's most happy work is only done
By sweet attraction to its sacred hearth,
To bless and warm the heart as the bright sun
Attracts and warms and beautifies the earth.

And such bright homes there were and some there are,
To which the heart will turn where'er we roam;
From distant years, from climes however far,
The sweet attraction draws us back to home.

Back to the happy hearth and haunts of childhood
I go in dreams to be again a boy,
To meet once more the blessed homestead angels
Who gave me drink from their own cup of joy.

Oft they divided with me their possessions,
And sang for me the sweetest songs they had,
Oft carried all my foolish cares of childhood,
And smiled away the thoughts that made me sad.

Oh, how I loved them when I heard their voices
Along the gentle brooks and in the trees,
Now singing with the birds, now with the waters,
Then with the plaintive spirits of the breeze.

On winter evenings round the cheerful fireside
I felt their glowing cheeks against my own,
And bowing by the blessed domestic altar
I heard them whisper of the heavenly throne.

Ofttimes I heard them in my mother's stanzas
While singing as a mother only sings,
And as my eyelids closed they sat beside her,
And covered me, while sleeping, with their wings.

I saw them in my playmates' happy faces,
If angels ever look from mortal eyes,
And when one died, my infant faith assured me
She'd gone home with the angels to the skies.

Oh, happy then was I with home and kindred,
By winter's hearth or summer's fragrant grove,

Each part of my sweet home seemed part of
heaven,
So well the angels wove their spell of love.

WINTER VANQUISHED.

So come! let 's take my nag of a rhyme,
And gallop back to the good old time
When blazing fire on homestead hearth
Made it the dearest spot on earth.

What though stern Winter, grim and old,
Came riding in his chariot cold,
Clothed in his ermine-robes of snow,
With crown of ice upon his brow,
With beard of frost so white and grand,
An icicle sceptre in his hand,
To sit like a tyrant on his throne,
And rule as though the world were his own?
What though the earth grew stiff and dead
Under the frost-king's fearful tread,
And every tree and shrub and flower
Succumbed beneath his blighting power,
And asked in vain, with suppliant mien,
He 'd spare their beauteous robes of green
And crimson, purple and rich brown,
Nor hurl to dust their glorious crown,

Richer than monarch's diadem,
Which generous Autumn gave to them?
The tyrant had no power to blight
The roses in the homestead bright.
If the old, stern chap entered our portals
We made him caper with us mortals,
Softened him down as man of snow
Melts 'neath the sun's round face aglow;
His nostril-blasts blew not more rough
Than old man's from a pinch of snuff,
And all his vassals howled in vain
Like hungry wolves at window-pane.
For blazing logs on honest hearth
Filled up our homes with summer mirth,
And beasts of prey always retire
Before the searching eye of fire.
We braved him in his own domain,
On lake where he had fixed his chain,
And underneath his storm-filled cloud,
Where his trumpeters blew shrill and loud,
With blasts of biting air and sleet,
His triumph o'er the earth at his feet,
Which lay like a corpse in its shroud.
We braved him armed with skate and sled,
With hearts all warm and cheeks all red,
With laugh and shouts of girls and boys
We turned his doldrums into joys,
And changed his icy morsels cold

To spangling gems and glistening gold,
And from his windy chariot stole
His weapons sharp and cups of dole;
As Franklin, with a simple kite,
Disarmed the stormy Thunder-sprite,
And having his fierce lightnings gained,
Played with him as with tiger chained.

SKATING.

A PAIR of skates is a pair of wings!
How the gliding iron rings!
Like a bird that at once both flies and sings.
Onward we rush
Past hillock and bush,
Racing and chasing
And facing the wind,
Every nerve bracing,
Evolving, revolving,
Each one resolving
Not to be left behind,
And not to be outdone
In clangor and shouting and fun!
And many a manly fellow,
With honest hearts as mellow
As their hands are tough,
And their voices rough,

Draw little sleds behind them,
With little girls fast clinging,
And gallantly they mind them,
As they join their merry singing
Till the solemn woods are ringing,
And the ice-king's palace-floor
Shakes with the wild uproar!
So the gallant knights of old
When they took a castle bold,
Drank the wine of its captive king,
Made it merry with their bouts,
Made its dull walls crack and ring
With their laughter and their shouts.

THE RETURN.

WHILE revelling thus, oft would the flying light
Leave us unconscious of the darkening skies,
Till day had gone to bed and dusky night
Looked down upon us with her starry eyes.

Then we, well weary with our wholesome sport,
With simple farewells take our several ways,
And homeward bound, like ships that make for port,
We hail the beacons of our hearth's bright blaze.

How they sparkle! how they burn!
How the laughing chimney roars
Now to welcome our return
From the winter out of doors!
The gladdening beams look out to see us come,
And smile with joy to have us home again,
Glowing with delight,
Looking through the window-pane,
Dancing at the garden-gate.

So children at evening their father await,
The fire in their young hearts burning;—
They watch at the windows all restless with bliss,
Each eager to catch the first sight;—
At length when they see him returning
They shout with delight,
And rush with their might
Over the floor,
Out of the door,
Into their father's arms for a kiss,
At the garden-gate.

Or like the warm words on the lips of a maiden,
The burning coals of her love,
Whose heart with sad fear has been long sore laden,

Whose prayers have been heard above;
She sees her sea-tossed rover,
And springs to the arms of her lover,
At the garden-gate,
And the words of her welcome are coals of love
To her lover's heart at the garden-gate.

FORECAST.

Such happy welcome ever waits
Where wisdom guards the garden-gates,
Where men have heard what seers say, —
"In Summer work for Winter's day."
But cold the welcome, cold the hearth,
And cold as death the lips of mirth,
When they return who have not heard
The faithful prophet's warning word.
There dwells a seer in the wood
Whom wise men question for their good;
Lithe-limbed though gray; so known to fame
There is no need to name his name.
His oracle men search to know,
The Winter's length and depth of snow;
And like some human weather-clerks
He gives them good and bad by jerks.
A cold, round winter he foretells
By double stores of nuts, whose shells

Are doubly thick, by strange forecast,
As if to shield them from the blast;
He lines his house with extra walls,
With quiet foresight barring squalls,
Gets extra blankets for his bed,
And guards the roof which shields his head.
  Woe to the man who will not hear
The warnings of this gray old seer!
Woe to his house when wintry day
Swoops like an eagle on its prey,
And holds it bound, in icy clasp,
More strongly than an eagle's grasp!
Or when its far-stretched, stormy wing,
Casts its cold shadows on the Spring.
  Than these far happier, wiser they
Who heed what faithful prophets say,
And warning take of evil day.
For them armed Forecast drives off fear,
And breaks the rough terrors of the year;
When like fierce rushing Philistines,
The storms come down on roofs and vines,
He, armed with club and crowned with corn,
Has Samson's strength ere he was shorn.

THE WOODMAN'S AXE.

Thanks to the sickle and the plough
Which wove the corn-wreath for his brow!
Thanks for the axe whose hardy blows
Wrought out the arms which quell his foes!
Thanks for the sickle and the plough,
But let them rest, they need it now;
And let the tough axe brave the snow
And meet the winds with blow for blow,
To keep the hearthstone in a glow.
His heaviest strokes he ever wields
When Winter binds the furrowed fields;
Else might the tyrant bind us too,
And with his ice-spears pierce us through.
But well he fears, as well he knows,
The hardy woodman's sturdy blows.
He wisely toils who grinds the axe
Ere the huge forest he attacks,
And rises early with the horn
Of chanticleer who brings the morn;
Then braced and cheered with smoking meal
Crunches the ground with hastening heel,
And works all day without a noon,
Else shortening days bring night too soon;
And these are days when flowing blood
Forsakes the winter-stricken wood,

And favor well-directed skill
Which would not hurt what it must kill.
  Where the huge trees lie felled and prone
There leave their headless trunks alone,
And homeward first draw lighter loads,
Unless the snow now strews the roads;
When the great logs at length must go,
The ox will thank you for the snow.
  Thus patient toil till you have drawn
A full year's stock, and cleft and sawn,
(For wedge and saw must help the while,)
And housed it safely, pile on pile;
Then leave it sheltered from the sky
Till thirsty March-winds lick it dry;
Or leave it for the coming year;
Of present hoard give ample cheer.
This is the wisdom of the axe,
Forestalling Winter's fierce attacks,
By homely toil and common sense,
Shrewd forecast and kind Providence.

  Thanks for the axe! pile up the fire,
And let the rising flames rise higher!
Pile on the logs and let them dance
Till the bright day of Spring advance!
  Thanks for the axe! it clears the way
For yet more glorious, brighter day!
Oh, crack not only Winter's crown,

But hack the thrones of tyrants down!
Clear the glad way for gold-haired Mirth
To smile on every poor man's hearth;
Through forests old and morass dun
Cleave a bright pathway for the sun;
Scoop out from tangled copse and trees
Ripe harvest-fields to wave like seas;
And for a nation's steady tracks
Hew out the way, oh, mighty axe!
For peace and truth and freedom's sway
Hew, mighty axe! the great highway!
Strike hard till every tyrant reels!
Strike hard till Earth, unshackled, feels
The rolling of Christ's chariot-wheels!

THE SONG OF THE AXE.

Oh, a loyal thing is the woodman's axe,
  And a terror to freemen's foes,
For it clears the path for a nation's tracks
  As the empire Westward goes.

Oh, a thing of joy is the woodman's axe,
  For it makes the old homestead bright,
And it sees that the hearthstone never lacks
  Good heart of a cold, dreary night.

Oh, a sturdy thing is the woodman's axe,
  And the sturdy woodman's hard blows
Make his arms as strong as the wood he hacks,
  And his cheeks as red as a rose.

In the early morn o'er the crusted snow
  To the woods he hastens away,
And you hear the steady blow upon blow
  Of his good, sharp axe all the day.

The tall, old trees, who 've swayed in the breeze,
  And have braved a thousand fierce storms,
Are losing their strength by sure degrees,
  At each stroke of the woodman's arms.

Hark! the rebound of a crashing sound!
  'T is another old oak gone down,
Bearing his satellites crushed to the ground,
  Like a king when he loses his crown.

Before the strong woodman's axe they 're dumb,
  Their tough hearts of oak shake with fears,
And one by one they 're forced to succumb, —
  These braves of a hundred long years.

And all the day long they 're strewn along,
  Like huge giants slain in a fight,

And the woodman hacks away with a song,
  For he thinks of his home and the night.

At his home awaits, by the garden-gates,
  His pet little girl with her sled,
And on the pond his boys with their skates,
  And their cheeks are all rosy red.

Within his own doors o'er the oaken floors
  The old hearthstone is laughing and bright,
And the honest wife, whom he almost adores,
  Will welcome him home with delight.

Oh, a thing of strength is the woodman's axe!
  For it brightens the faces at home,
And opens the paths for an empire's tracks
  In the future ages to come.

PARADISE LOST.

  Labor and forethought, one on either side,
Will take a poor man oft with steady stride
Up to the golden palaces of kings; —
Such wealth and honor, frugal labor brings; —
While wealthy sloth brings woeful waste and want,
Turns plenty out and brings in famine gaunt,

Brings down the rich to take the poor man's
seat,
Without his strength the poor man's fate to
meet, —
So powerless hoarded wealth to guard and
bless
Whom sloth and sin lead down to wretched-
ness.

Upon a hill-side, near its summit, stood
A mansion skirted by an ancient wood,
Whose veteran trees, like soldiers in array,
Stood sentinel to guard it night and day;
From fierce assaults of winds and winter storms
They interposed, like shields, their faithful
forms;
On these they caught hot Summer's hissing
darts,
Nor shunned to brave the lightning to their
hearts, —
The lightning-bolts which else had struck it
down; —
It stood thus guarded like a kingdom's crown.
Far northward giant mountains rose to sight,
Now draped in clouds, now wearing robes of
light;
Southward a valley, which, in summer dress,
Could have no rival for its loveliness; —

Green meadows, fruitful fields, and gardens lay
Upon its bosom all the summer-day,
Nor lack within that house of costliest things
Which art creates or busy commerce brings;
Gay troops of friends sat often at its board
To catch the golden smiles of its gay lord;
A gentle wife, both beautiful and good,
Of word refined and not an action rude,
Whose sweet expression made assurance sure
That in her heart could dwell no thought impure;
They prayed, who saw her almost angel face,
That there no bitter tears might leave their trace;
And children healthful, sprightly, such as make
The parents love each other for their sake;
Four opening buds through which the rising day
Poured light and beauty with its quickening ray;
They both their parents' images combined,
Their father's princely form and earnest mind,
Their mother's heart like gold from heaven refined.

What more could mortal ask of earthly bliss
Save heavenly guard to shield his happiness?
Such guard was lacking and insidious vice
Entered that house, as Satan Paradise.

At those grand feasts there sat a skeleton;
Within the wine-cup where its color shone
Like a bright ruby in a costly ring,
There lurked a serpent with a deadly sting,
Whose venom once infused no mortal can
Retain the glory of the fated man.
He who so princely sat and passed the wine
Now feels its sting and wallows with the swine;
The majesty has left his lofty brow;
No kingly reason sits enthroned there now.
Like him of old whom unclean spirits drove
From common haunts of men and home of love
To dwell among the tombs, and none could
tame,
So he, possessed and burned with inward flame,
Asunder breaks the chains and cords that bind
The loving heart of man to human kind;
He cuts himself with stones, and bleeds and
foams,
Among the tombs of dead affections roams;
By evil spirits driven to and fro,
From sin to sin, from woe to deeper woe.
How dark the night when such a sun has set!
How drear the home where once such pleas-
ures met!
How black the hearthstone where such ruddy
flame
Once turned the night to day when Winter
came.

Yet not the thunderbolt and lightning flash
Brought down that mansion with a sudden crash;
The demon first could scarce an entrance gain,
Then one by one brought others in his train,
And by degrees fixed there his subtle reign.
They put their heels upon the cheerful hearth,
Its fires went out, hushed were its songs of mirth;
They cast vile shadows on its daily bread,
Destroyed the relics of its blessed dead,
Dissolved its pearls within the fatal cup
And bade their victim drink the jewels up,
Consumed its beauty, scattered all its gold,
Sent blight and sickness in the sacred fold,
And the torn lambs were shivering in the cold.
Their poor wan mother sits to watch and weep,
Or sings with broken heart her lambs to sleep,
And waits for his return, who, well she knows,
Will meet her kind caress with cruel blows.
At last the demons turn them out of door, —
They and their children to return no more.
The troops of friends who graced their princely board,
To catch the golden smiles of its gay lord,
Do not go down to cheer the lowly cot,
Whose humble walls now close around his lot.

They ate his bread, they drank his golden cup,
And saw him fall but do not lift him up.
Such friends are eagles gathered to the prey,
Which eat the carcass clean, then fly away;
Or swarms of insects in a moment flown
When all the sweets on which they sipped are gone.
But though our friends forsake, our vices cling,
Disguising still the ruin which they bring.
His followed him, with promise false and fair,
To cover all his shame and drown his care;
They led him blinded to the gulf of sin,
And bound him hand and foot and plunged him in.

AN ANGEL.

Then though all men forsook their fallen friend,
A bright-eyed angel watched him to the end,
And fanned the embers on his blackened hearth
To bring dead hope to life with second birth.
Though bound by demons hand to foot, and cast
In outer darkness where they held him fast,
One heart still searched him out where'er he went,

Like mercy after some lost spirit sent,
To bring him back to heaven a penitent;
That heart, though bruised and trampled in
the dust,
Still like the vine would cling, with patient
trust,
And hold him with the tendrils of its love,
And upward climb to bear him up above.
Oh, faithful wife, oh, loving heart and true!
What thou canst not what could an angel do?
He heard that loving one with earnest tone
Plead like a sobbing child with God alone.
He heard? God heard, and answered with a
dart
From heaven which pierced his broken heart;
A broken heart gives entrance to a Guest
Who heals its wounds and gives the weary
rest.
Oh, had that lofty house received but Him!
Its fires had not gone out, its lights grown dim.
No home, no heart is safe from curse and sin
That will not hear Him knock and let Him in.

THE DELIVERER.

O WEARY heart, O heart oppressed with sin,
O'erwhelmed with sense of danger and despair,
Unbolt thy door and let the Saviour in,
And cast on Him the burden of thy care.

Long hath He stood at thy unopened gate, —
Through many a weary day and lagging night, —
And knocked in vain and yet doth vainly wait,
To take thy load and make thy burden light.

Why longer sit in unavailing grief,
When One so ready stands to give thee rest?
Arise! unlock thy door, and sweet relief
Shall enter in with thy Almighty Guest.

Then shall He sup with thee and thou with Him,
And in that feast of love new life be thine;
And thou shalt see with eyes no longer dim
Thy Saviour Guest all lovely and divine.

Thy dark, cold chambers He shall reillume
And warm with coals from heavenly hills brought down,

Whose fires celestial burn but not consume,
And many waters cannot quench nor drown.

PARADISE REGAINED.

Oh, patient woman! oh, long-suffering wife!
Your prayers and tears, by angels borne on high,
Have been for him the messengers of life,
And come again with tokens from the sky.

The fiends exorcised, and his soul set free,
And frugal plenty on his humble board,
His happy children climbing on his knee, —
Oh, faithful wife, how great is your reward!

A new and happy man, by heavenly birth,
He lives again to bless you all your days;
The cheerful fires shall blaze upon your hearth,
And Heaven receive your cheerful songs of praise.

Behold their happy dwelling! mark the scene!
A wreath of joy encircles that sweet brow!
She sits enthroned more lovely than a queen,
And love's own sceptre sways and rules there now.

There where the demons raged within its walls, —
The fiends that lurk in the inebriate's cup, —
And turned her husband out to drunken brawls,
And burned his love and all her dower up.

Her children frightened when their father came,
Would hush their little songs and hide away;
She met him with a smile to give, — and shame!
He ate the meal for which she toiled all day.

Though fainting 'neath her burden, she arose
Heroically and bore it yet again;
Returned caresses for his cruel blows,
And wept in secret to conceal her pain.

Oh, patient woman! your long-suffering love
At length has clasped from death your risen lord;
Your hearthstone glows, your songs are heard above;
Oh, faithful wife, how great is your reward.

THE LOST HOME-FIRES.

FAR happier she in action and in fate
From one I knew, whose sharp and grievous word,
By slow degrees, turned all her love to hate,
And digged a gulf betwixt herself and lord.

At first she loved him, left her home for his,
Hiding her eyes from his deficiencies,
And found in all around her source of bliss,
As flowers give sweets to working honey-bees.

More like a child than wife, indulged, caressed,
Joy after joy came knocking at their door;
Wealth did what wealth can do to make them blessed,
And children played, like sunbeams, on their floor.

An angry spirit ruled her husband oft,
Like one possessed against his better will,
Which fled before a soothing answer soft,
Like word of Christ which bade the storm be still.

Oh, had the storm which lowered on their path
Been always met by sweet and pleasant word, —
By answer soft that turned away his wrath, —
She had not slain her love, nor slain her lord.

But anger fed by anger grew to hate —
A wall of fire 'twixt them and happiness,
Like angry flames that stood at Eden gate
To bar our parents from their former bliss.

The home-fires died that once burned clear and bright,
Only black embers smouldered on the hearth;
And songs which warbled from the heart's delight,
Were frozen on the dead, cold lips of mirth.

Poor wife! from graves of garnered joys she fled,
Nor happier then, still followed by the rod:
Poor man! his heart, his love, his hope all dead,
He quenched his hearth's last spark in his own blood!

BURIED ALIVE.

ALAS, that tale like this should e'er be true!
That dead tied to the living e'er should be!
A weary burden all their journey through,
Unless some friendly knife shall cut them free.

How many marble prisons there are built
By name of palaces, whose polished cell
And painted walls could tell such tales of guilt,
Would make us blush if they had tongues to tell.

The costliest mansions bought with human loves
No more than polished prisons e'er can be, —
Rich gold-barred cages filled with wounded doves,
Which mourn and moan in vain for liberty.

Alas, what gorgeous sepulchres they are!
Where human beings, buried when alive,
Sit down and mope in doleful, dull despair,
Or with their fate in madness fiercely strive.

SLEEPY HOLLOW.

But we will leave these dismal walls
Where sadness like a shadow falls,
And wealth and misery unite
The flowers of human love to blight, —
These gilded homes of pomp and pride,
Where folly, guilt, and woes abide,
And Christ, who outside stands and waits,
Is driven from the palace-gates,
Though standing there, with thorn-scarred head,
To heal their sick and raise their dead.

We 'll hasten from such scenes of blight
To those shall rest our weary sight, —
Where we can see the hills and trees,
And feel the free-winged, healthful breeze,
And tread the paths, in vale and glen,
Where human love still lives with men,
And where the hearthstone, pure and bright,
Fills happy homes with joyous light.

North of the great Metropolis,
A score of miles, in rural bliss,
Where Hudson, famed for glorious waves,
His Eastern banks with kisses laves,

Lies Sleepy Hollow, known to fame
As drowsy land by drowsy name; —
A land it is of sweet repose,
When Summer smiles, or Winter blows;
Asleep to that which murders sleep, —
Ambition with it's dizzy steep,
And love of gold's great shining heap;
Awake to all that waking eyes
And honest hearts should love to prize.

IRVING.

I NEED not tell
How Irving wove a wizard spell,
With warp and woof of truth and jest,
O'er that sweet vale of living rest:
Irving, now numbered with the blessed,
O'er whose green grave a nation mourns,
Whose pen a nation's life adorns,
Whose words of wisdom, winged with mirth,
Fly evermore round all the earth,
Unchecked by wintry frosts of time,
To cheer the homes of every clime;
For whom a world may well bewail, —
But, peace! he sleeps in yon sweet vale!
It bears his name on every breeze,
And graven on its rocks and trees;

Nor could do less and yet approve
That love is just return of love.
He gave its rocks and nooks a name
Which else had been unknown to fame,
And sent it forth, from child to sage,
To make its paths a pilgrimage;
He touched the valley with his pen
And lo! it teemed with living men;
His pen, a weird magician's wand,
He stretched across the Sleepy Land,—
The Land, from sleep of ages free,
Awoke to immortality!
Pocantico still rolls his stream
Beneath the bridge of Irving's dream,
As when he heard the tramp and scream
Of Ichabod, that fearful night,
When Brom Bones gave him such a fright;
And who would not feel some alarm
To see a man's head 'neath his arm?—
A pumpkin-head can do some harm;
And who would stand and dare combat him
If he should take and throw it at him?
Brom Bones, his well-made pumpkin-head
Beneath his arm, with steady tread
Overtook the lean-shanked Ichabod,
Just at tne bridge, where oft had trod
The headless horseman, and at once
Hurled pumpkin-head against the dunce;

His rival fell; — the winged blind-god
Flew from the heart of Ichabod;
Katrina took the dauntless Brom,
And many Brom Bones sprang therefrom.

THE OLD GRAVEYARD.

The rivals sleep. And with them he whose
wand
Hath made their names so famous in the
land;
By the Old Church they sleep,
Beyond death's stream,
No more to laugh and weep,
No more to dream.

With thousands in God's Acre they repose,
Where the hushed wind in gentlest whispers
blows,
And just beyond their graves
The flowing river,
With never-ceasing waves,
Flows on forever.

THE OLD CHURCH.

THE Old Church long has stood,—
  For ages may it stand,
Storehouse of heavenly food,
  And light-house of the land.

Within its sacred walls
  What thousands, now asleep
Where its blessed shadow falls,
  Have bowed to pray and weep!

Old Church, with doctrines old
  As God's eternal truth,
Within its sacred fold
  Men still renew their youth.

Ages have rolled along
  Since yonder Hudson's waves
First heard its holy song,
  First saw its opened graves.

Still in its water-springs,
  Whose streams are never dry,
Hope bathes her drooping wings,
  And gathers strength to fly.

Still from its tower of light
The radiant truth is given,
To cheer men through the night,
And guide them on to heaven.

Church of my fathers, venerable pile!
Ages have passed away while thou hast stood,
A monument of Heaven's approving smile
On the enduring virtues of the good.

Forgetful of their cunning are the hands,
And cold the hearts whose faith and strength were given
To rear thy precious stones and golden sands,
Thou holy House of God, thou Gate of Heaven!

They sleep beside thee in thy sacred ground;
Moss-covered gravestones tell us where they lie;
But yet they live and in thy walls are found;
While thou remainest they can never die.

When Freedom called them from their peaceful fields,
They freely gave their treasure and their blood;

Then came to thee with honored swords and
shields,
To give the praise of triumph to their God.

The locust-grove that heard their Sabbath-song,
Through open windows, on a summer day,
Still casts its cooling shadows soft along
The holy men who at thy altars pray.

The gentle stream whose mellow voice they
heard,
Still flows before thy door; and while it stirs
The lily on its banks, still, like a bird,
Pours forth its music with thy worshippers.

And yonder stands the mill, old-timed and good,
That ground our father's grain and gave
them bread;
But thou, O mill of God! didst give them food
Which will not let them die, though they are
dead.

THE OLD HOMESTEAD.

WITHIN a mile of this old, sacred place,
Has stood a farm-house since the year of grace,
Beyond the memory of the oldest man;

'Twas built at various times, without a plan,
Perhaps by different owners, or by one
At different times, part after part was done,
Thus growing with the owner's growing purse,
Beginning small; men in our day do worse;
Reverse this prudent order right about,
And so, like wasps, are biggest when first out.
What fires in winter blazed upon its hearth!
Such brave, old Christmas times, and Christmas mirth,
And Christmas-trees, and Christmas evergreens,
And romps, and rounds of games, and Christmas scenes;
Such good old chimneys, where was ample room
For Santa Claus, and where he loved to come:
That homely Homestead was indeed a home.
Near by stood barns and granaries and racks,
So full it seemed they 'd burst; and rows of stacks;
And flocks of sheep; and generous cows, whose milk
Was milk, and whose bright coats were soft as silk;
And horses which a child might dare to pat,—
Kind horses, not so very fast, but fat;
And patient oxen, meek and gentle-eyed,
Such as great Webster, just before he died,
So longed to see once more, and called them friends,—

His "*honest* friends." Thus rural life still
blends
The love of country with the love of home,
As with the greatest statesmen of old Rome.

THE HOUSE-DOG.

And there was "Range," the house-dog,
last, not least;
The faithful mastiff was a noble beast, —
Old Range who loved the children so, and
hauled
Their little sleds, as harmless when they mauled
And pulled his ears, as when they gave him
bread
And meat and stroked his lofty head;
Why should not Ranger have a little space,
As faithful watch and guardian of the place,
Since men less worthy have an honored mound,
Who were not, like old Ranger, faithful found?

THE FATHER.

Some men's great virtues first begin to bloom
Upon the marble which o'ertops their tomb.
Not so with him who ruled that humble home,
And made it happier than a prince's dome.

His bloomed in childhood, ripened with his
prime,
And bore rich fruits through all his life and
time.
He first was known as an obedient son,
Who loved his parents, loved by every one;
Then as a husband, faithful, kind, and true;
Then as a neighbor, giving each his due;
Then as a father, ruling well his own;
Through all a humble Christian he was known,
Whose good example was an orb of light,
To cheer the sad and set the erring right.

THE MOTHER.

The mother of the household was the wife
Whom Solomon describes, whose heart and life
Look well unto her house, in blessed employ,
A virtuous woman and a crown of joy.
"The land needs mothers!" said a statesman
wise,
Who saw the future with far-reaching eyes;
Our happy country had good mothers then,
The land was safe, for angels walked with men!

THE GIRLS.

THEIRS were the children which King David's pen
Has placed within the homes of happy men.
The girls, in old times, were not born to shirk
The wholesome duties of the household work;
Nor did they fear the sun and open air
To keep their sweet complexions soft and fair,
And bleach the roses white which God made red;
Nor was their only prayer how they might wed.

THE BOYS.

THE fathers taught their sons to guide the plough,
And walk erect with manly step and brow;
The sons grew stalwart in the open fields,
And plucked the fruits which honest labor yields;
The Summer's labor brought the Winter's cheer,
And Plenty ne'er forsook them all the year;
They braved the toil and reaped the toil's reward,

Which filled their barns and spread their
ample board;
And busy hands they cheered with merry
tongue,
By singing this or some like rural song: —

THE WORK-SONG.

Up and away!
The sun shines bright;
Work in the day,
Sleep in the night.

While sluggards sleep
The rank weeds grow,
Harvests they reap
Who plough and sow.

Drones increase sorrow;
Lazily they
Leave till to-morrow
Work of to-day.

Wretched the shirkers!
Joyous are we;
Happy the workers,
Healthy and free!

Farmers go singing
  Forth to their farms,
Glad they come, bringing
  Sheaves in their arms.

Hoping, the sower
  Soweth the seed;
Joyful, the mower
  Moweth the mead.

Smoothly the plough
  Turns the sod over,
Row after row,
  Covering the clover.

Soon the corn springs, —
  (Law is not fickle);
Soon the heart sings,
  Plying the sickle.

Borne on the gales,
  Sound clear and sweet
Thresher's loud flails
  Threshing the wheat.

Threshers keep time,
  Steady and strong,
Flailing the rhyme
  Of a rustic song.

Laughing, the grain
  Leaps from the sheaves, —
Falls as the rain
  Falls on the leaves.

Hark! how the mill,
  Sunshine or rain,
Works with a will,
  Grinding the grain!

Round goes the wheel,
  Covered with foam;
Out comes the meal
  On its way home.

Smiles the old miller
  In the mill-door,
Fills up the tiller, —
  Thinks of the poor.

Labor has song,
  Labor has health;
Labor is strong,
  Labor is wealth.

Sloth addeth sorrow
  Under the sun;
Sluggards still borrow
  Woes which they shun.

Work addeth pleasures,
  Bringeth forth mirth,
Scattereth treasures
  Over the earth.

Up, then, away!
  The sun shines bright;
Work in the day!
  Sleep in the night!

INDUSTRY.

SUCH was their toil; not that which frets the life
  With love of gold, which eats the heart away;
Nor labor weary with its life-long strife
  To keep the wolves of poverty at bay.

All day the industrious, busy hum was heard,
  No idle mind, no idle hand was there;
They caught the music of the early bird,
  They drank the freshness of the dewy air.

Thus nursed by manly toil for usefulness,
  Each mind well-stored and disciplined the while,
Each sunlit heart disposed to cheer and bless,
  Each sun-browned face benignant with a smile, —

They gave their labor to the plough and field,
And these returned rich harvests for their work, —
For mother earth delights her wealth to yield
To skill and toil which neither doubt nor shirk.

They gave their counsels and their aid to men, —
The poor, the wandering, and unfortunate, —
And in their turn received from heaven again
In measure double on their soul's estate.

They gave their hearts to God, and in reward,
He walled them round against insidious vice,
And made their hearts like gardens of the Lord,
Whose fruits and flowers still grow in Paradise.

Their house hospitable, with open gate,
Gave hearty welcome, with its generous store,
To rich and poor alike, to small and great,
And Friendship's path led straight unto their door.

Oh, happy rural life to hearts content!
Oh, happy men, who sing away their cares!
Stern Winter pinches the improvident,
But lavishes good cheer on toil like theirs.

Thus, when rude blasts came howling from the
North,
And Night sat longest on the frozen earth,
Their stores of plenty poured rich treasures
forth,
Like Joseph's granaries in time of dearth.

And when old Christmas, ushered in with
song,
Came smiling through the clouds and wintry
night,
To strew with gifts his pathway all along,
Their home seemed brightest e'en where all
were bright.

There sits the old man in his easy-chair, —
Their father's father, full of merry mood;
They love and reverence his hoary hair, —
That crown of glory to the old and good.

For in those times in Holy Book they read,
What now the young too oft forget to scan,
"Thou shalt rise up before the hoary head,
And honor shalt the face of the old man."

THE GRANDFATHER.

AND now the little children
Come gathering round his chair;
They have a little frolic,
And wish to have him there.

He rises to go with them,
For he loves the children well,
And loves to tell the stories
They love to hear him tell.

He stands to watch their frolics,
While leaning on his staff;
Though weary, still he lingers
Where happy children laugh.

Their little merry voices,
Out-ringing in their play,
Bring back a troop of memories,
To cheer him on his way.

Sweet loves of little children
Are sunbeams round his heart,
They were the first to greet him,
They 'll be the last to part.

The path of life 's a circle,
  And he who farthest goes
On its mysterious journey,
  So mixed with joys and woes,

Will come where he first started, —
  First prattled, walked, and smiled, —
And, with his ripe experience,
  Will be once more a child.

THE DAY BEFORE CHRISTMAS.

AND merry grew the old man's heart,
And merry the house in every part:
Merry the old, merry the young;
Merry the heart, merry the tongue;
Merry the hearth with merry flame,
When Christmas, merry Christmas came! —
Christmas, the merriest day of the year,
With right good will and right good cheer!
  The day before was busiest day,
For merriest one preparing way.
Busy for body and for mind;
How the old spice-mills grind and grind!
Thousands of raisins inside out!
Doughnuts frying, bobbing about;
Many a hand in sweetened dough;
Hot ovens, filled with row on row

Of fruit-cake, pound-cake, all sorts of pies,
Blister the cook and roast her eyes;
Many a hen-roost suffers attack,
Many a duck has quacked his last quack,
Many a cock has fought his last foe,
And woke next morn to crow his last crow;
And many a gobbler 's gobbled his last
That merry Christmas may not fast.

The work flies on, down leaps the sun,
But much hard work must yet be done.
Old Weather, much-abused good chap,
Whom all delight to cuff and rap,
Himself has busy chores to do: —
Must hang up curtains black and blue,
And dress out trees with jewels bright
To flash and gleam in Christmas light;
Must make up drizzle, sleet, and snow,
And hurry up in doing so,
And rattle, slam, and bang, and blow!
Must weave o'er fields his wicker-work,
And not stand still, not try to shirk,
But work, and work, and work, and work!
Like woman who is never done
From rising till the setting sun.
No time for rest, for he must bake
The whole round earth into a cake, —
A Christmas-cake, all smooth and nice,
With not a crack in its frosting of ice.

Old Weather 's a jolly chap that night,
Working for Christmas with his might!
If he meet a man with a sour face,
Moping along at surly pace,
Growling like cross-grained dog or cat,
And finding fault with this or that, —
At Christmas sports and Christmas grace, —
He wallops him into a race,
Springs round a corner on his back,
And starts him with a sudden whack!
Then roars and races like a pack
Of howling wolves upon his track;
He hurls great snowballs in his face,
To hurry up his lagging pace;
Shakes down a tree-full on his head
To make for him a hasty bed,
Then trips his heels and lays him flat;
Blinds both his eyes, staves in his hat,
Rings his red ears, bites all his toes,
Benumbs his chin, and nips the tip
Of Sour Crout's nose.
And serves him right!
For on such a night
No one 's a right
To be at all glum,
Or mum!
Oh, the Weather 's a jolly chap in his way,
A-getting folks ready for Christmas-day.

CHRISTMAS-EVE.

Now around the fire sitting,
Father smoking, mother knitting,
Nimble needles quickly plying,
In the happy hour fast flying;
Grandpa in his corner musing,
Now and then a word infusing
Of the long, long past Decembers,
Which he now so well remembers;
Speaks of them who filled the places
Filled now by these happy faces,
With a gentle tone of sadness
Mingling with his words of gladness;
But the yule-log burning brightly
Warms his lips with thoughts more sprightly;
Fire-beams on the walls are dancing,
Imps on fairy-horses prancing;
On the hearth-stone chestnuts roasting;
Apples ditto, simmering, toasting,
Singing, blushing, swaying, stuttering,
Bursting with warm feelings, sputtering,
Ever-smiling faces turning,
Like good martyrs, at the burning!
Children watch, with faces glowing,
Round the hearth-stone, each one showing
Which are his and which the others,

Which are grandpa's, father's, mother's;
Which are for the little sister,
Who, her face almost a blister,
Perseveres in getting nigher
Every minute to the fire,
All impatient for the treasure,
All aglow with anxious pleasure,
And her little childish prattling,
Helps along the noise and rattling.
What with these, and games, and singing,
Each his share of pleasure bringing,
Each to please the other trying,
Oh, the time is swiftly flying!

Now Jake, the hired man, had heard
From some old joker, on his word,
Which he esteemed as true as steel,
That all the cows were sure to kneel,
And cocks to crow, with all their might,
Some hour upon that blessed night,
'Tween Christmas-eve and Christmas-morn,
To show the hour when Christ was born.
So went to see the wondrous sight
Was sure to happen on that night,
And stayed with cattle till content,
Then came as wise as when he went,
But with his beard turned ghostly white,
Changed in that time, — but not by fright; —

Jack Frost had painted it in jest,
And pinned it to his woollen vest,
To show the boys how frost or fright
Will change a fiery beard to white,
As we oft see, by weird attack,
A red or graybeard changed to black!

THE EVENING PRAYER.

But now the hour draws near for prayer; —
The father takes, with reverent air,
The Holy Book from well-known place,
And reads, with inward prayer for grace,
The holy Gospel's wondrous story, —
How angels from the realms of glory
Appeared and sang at Jesus's birth, —
"Good will to man and peace on earth."
Then, each one kneeling by his chair,
The patriarch leads the evening prayer;
With earnest heart, and simple word,
And tremulous lips, he thanks the Lord
He had to one so old as he,
And sinful, as he grieved to be,
By blood-bought mercy given leave
To see another Christmas-eve.
And oh, to Heaven what praise there goes,
Like fragrance from a broken rose,

From the old patriarch's trembling prayer,
For those who bow beside him there,
His children and their children fair.
With simple, child-like form of speech,
Which never fails God's ear to reach,
He prays that He who came to earth
To take our form, by human birth,
And knew the feelings of a child,
And taught, and died, and reconciled
Offended Heaven and sinful man,
Would by redeeming love and plan,
Save him and his loved children all
From the sad ruin of the Fall, —
Bring him and his, their sins forgiven,
To the bright Homestead built in heaven;
And fill all years, and every clime,
With the good cheer of Christmas-time.

READY FOR SANTA CLAUS!

Early to bed on Christmas-eve!
Give Santa Claus time his gifts to leave;
Early to rise on Christmas-morn,
As soon as Chanticleer blows his horn!

Clean little stockings hung in rows,
Where the old hearth-stone smiling glows

On little bare feet as red as a rose,
While each, with earnest prattle, shows
What Santa Claus already knows, —
How to tell the one from the others,
So that next morn there 'll be no bothers;
At last, their little prayers all said,
They kiss good-night, and off to bed.

Early to bed, but not to sleep,
For little folk will vigils keep;
And too much joy, like too much sorrow,
Will make the heart long for the morrow;
And they who laugh, like those who grieve,
Can scarcely sleep on Christmas-eve.

Little eyes peeping behind the door,
Little feet pattering on the floor,
A sudden spring into little beds,
A covering up of little heads,
Show little folk have broke the laws,
And dared to watch for Santa Claus!

Wakeful still, they tell their stories,
Always childhood's wealth and glories;
Tales of terror, tales of wonder,
Almost rend their hearts asunder;
Each one in the weird rotation,
Tells by rote the strange relation;

Each believes, with faith unbroken,
Every wizard word that 's spoken;
They that tell and they that listen,
All alike with terror glisten,
And before the tales are ended,
Real and unreal all are blended:
Shadows turn to living creatures,
Horrible in form and features,
Murdering people for their riches,
And the house is filled with witches!
As they think their stories over,
Every head is under cover,
And the younger hugs the older
Vainly thinking him the bolder!
At length sleep comes and witches vanish,
And Christmas dreams all murderers banish.

THE HAPPY MAN.

Happy the man with such sweet household care!
Such lambs to shelter 'neath the old Homestead trees;
They fill his heart with all the joys they share,
And keep it young with childhood's memories.

Happy the man with wife, like fruitful vine,
Which for support clings to his stalwart form,
She, by a law as lovely as divine,
Shall hold him up when riven by the storm.

The growing fruit they nurse with so much care,
More precious in their eyes than finest gold,
And lovelier than costliest jewels are,
Will nourish them when they are sick or old.

Their sons shall be like plants grown in their youth,
Their daughters like the polished corner-stones
Of palaces, adorned with grace and truth,
Which kings might covet for their ivory thrones.

But hapless he who shuns the appointed wife; —
With none to bless him, none to call his own,
He only lives to prove, by dreary life,
"It is not good for man to be alone."

He spurns the best gift God to man has given,
His joy on earth and highest earthly crown;
She, like an angel, bears him up to heaven,
When evil spirits tempt to cast him down.

THE OLD BACHELOR.

WITHIN a lonely chamber,
  Without a fireplace,
There sits a lorn old bachelor,
  With long and dismal face.

He hugs the rusty air-tight,
  And lets the fire go out,
Then tries to blow it in again
  With 's mouth for bellows' spout.

"Oh, a merry man am I!"
  Thus sings the old bachelor,
Half in song and half a sigh; —
  He 'd sung so years before: —
"I 'd marry, but I dread it,
  I dread it more and more;
Yes, often have I said it,
  That marriage is a bore;
I 'll live until I die
  A happy bachelor!

"Oh, am I lonesome? No!
  I've not a chick to feed,
And have n't got to go
  A shopping till I bleed;

From all such matters free,
  From woman and her laws,
I 'm not compelled to be
  A sort of Santa Claus,
With lots of darned, old stockings
  Of saucy girls and boys,
On every Christmas hanging,
  For me to fill with toys.

"Am growing older? No!
  A man cannot grow old
Till married, then, you know,
  His years will all be told.
Pop Adam might have been
  In Paradise to-day,
Had Eve not took him in,
  By blabbing Satan's say!
I mean to keep my neck
  From such a noose as his,
Nor let a woman wreck
  My hope and happiness."

He thought the girls would jump
  A mile to have him, so
The question popped, and plump!
  The saucy girl said, No!
So he sold his wedding-suit,
  Called courtship all a bore,

And stays that dreadful brute,
  A sorry bachelor!

Like a walking ghost at night
  He haunts his silent room,
Draws all his curtains tight,
  Shuts in the evening gloom,
Then lights a tallow dip
  To mend his trousers by,
And takes a little nip
  Of something on the sly;
Soon takes another sip,
  Then another by and by;
He smacks his lonesome lip,
  Ends the evening with a sigh,
And prayers, of course, unsaid,—
  He thinks such things a bore,—
He tumbles into bed,
  A sorry bachelor!

THE HENPECKED.

NEXT door to him, and envious of his lot,
Like caged giraffe, by well-barred window sat
A tall, dejected, henpecked sort of man,
Who tried to sing, and thus his measures ran:—

"I envy the happy old bachelor
  Who sits by the window there,
So peacefully mending his trousers,
  With candle upon a chair.

"Oh, if he would only change places,
  To free me this Christmas-eve,
How gladly I 'd take his old trousers,
  And widow and children leave!

"I married my wife for a living,
  And such a living have I!
If I had to live it all over
  I think I would ask to die!

"I was young and she was a widow,
  And six nice children had she;
Her age was a very long forty,
  And mine a short twenty-three.

"But 'the years of her oldest cherub
  Would make our ages just even,'
She said; and she smiled like an angel
  That 's coaxing a sinner to heaven.

"And I was as long as a bean-pole,
  And she was as short as a tub;
But she said she 'liked a lean follow,—
  And did n't I like a dear chub?'

"And I was a mere counter-jumper,
  On thirty a month and the loot,
And she, — why she was a widow,
  With a house and fortune to boot!

"And she said, if I 'd be a lawyer
  She would marry me if I dare,
For a sprig of the law in her bosom
  The widow she wanted to wear.

"So I left the counter and studied
  Old Blackstone till I thought I 'd die;
But the widow patted my shoulder,
  And now, — yes! — a lawyer am I!

"And such a lawyer am I! — ah!
  With the widow, six children, and all
That a lawyer can eat, drink, and wear! ah!
  My share of said fortune is small.

"I think I 've the worst of said bargain,
  But the widow thinks otherwise,
As she hangs like a tub at my elbows,
  And languishes out of her eyes.

"I have to look down to behold her,
  As we walk together the street,
And the people smile on us passing,
  As the widow tries to look sweet.

5

"And likewise the widow's six children,
She calleth them all by my name,
As if I was the only husband
That ever got scorched in her flame.

"The people all look, and they wonder
That I — a young fellow like me —
Should be the affectionate father
Of children from thirteen to three.

"But so the good widow will have it,
And so must I have it also,
Or have a worse thing, she informs me,
Without my allowance to go!

"As sure as my name is 'U. William
Adolphus!' the husband of her,
I wish she again was a widow,
Or I was a widow–er!!"

TRUE LOVE.

While these twin doleful dirges sigh,
Like scudding clouds through cold night-air,
Bright stars look down from Christmas sky,
On happier hearts and scenes more fair.

Good Santa Claus o'er chimney-tops
Rides, hurrying on with sled and deer,
And where he sees a stocking, stops
To fill it up with Christmas cheer.

Though none have ever seen the saint,
All know he has a jolly face,
A body stout that cannot faint,
And gifts enough for all the race.

He to the Homestead drawing near,
Which many a year he 'd made rejoice,
Stopped suddenly, as if to hear
The words of some familiar voice.

It was the old man's song of love,
His song who led the evening prayer,
Who seemed to 've called one from above,
And sang as if he saw her there.

She long had filled his home with light,
A true wife to true husband given,
Until, to make e'en heaven more bright,
The Lord had taken her to heaven.

But that was only brighter home,
And near to this, though far above,
And so from heaven she 'd often come,
To listen to his song of love.

THE OLD MAN'S LOVE-SONG.

"This hair, which once was black, my love,
  Has turned to snowy white,
And these fond eyes that beamed on thee
  Have lost their glowing light.

"My vigorous limbs that sprang with life,
  Like birds in time of song,
And the blood that bounded through my veins
  Now slowly lag along.

"The May of life has gone, my love,
  The summer months have fled,
And birds that sang are silent now,
  And flowers that bloomed are dead.

"But though life's May has gone, my love,
  And though my hair is gray,
And though the light that cheered my eyes
  And thine has passed away,

"Yet is my heart as warm, my love,
  And beats for thee as brave
As ere my life had lost its youth,
  Or thou hadst found thy grave.

"And still I see thy radiant form
 That to these arms was given,
And thy sweet smiles yet warm my heart,
 Like sunbeams sent from heaven.

"And thine own words — I hear them yet —
 Fall fresh upon my ear,
As when at first thy lips confessed
 That I to thee was dear.

"Long years, — long years since then have fled,
 But love has been the same
As though thou hadst not joined the dead,
 But lived to fan the flame.

"The world will soon unchain me, love,
 And when my soul is free
They 'll lay my body in thy grave,
 And I will fly to thee!"

SANTA CLAUS.

Good Santa Claus heard this song through,
Then cracked his whip and away he flew!
For he had many gifts to strew,
And working hours were growing few;

But though he strewed his gifts like rain,
And scattered them from main to main,
None was more dear, of all he gave,
Than that sweet vision of the grave.

Early to bed on Christmas-eve!
Give Santa Claus time his gifts to leave!
Early to rise on Christmas morn!
As soon as chanticleer sounds his horn!

His clarion sounds that morning clear,
And earliest far of all the year;
And little ears are sharp to hear
His welcome call to Christmas cheer;

And long before the lagging sun
His good day's work has yet begun,
The little tongues are running fast,
Wondering how long the night will last.

Wondering if Santa Claus has been,
And why it is he can't be seen,
And if one listening might not hear
At least the bells on his reindeer.

They listen, — and good chanticleer
Rings in the morning loud and clear,
And little ears now feast upon
The music of his clarion.

Bare little feet are on the floor,
Little night-gowns flit through the door,
Little and big are on the run,
Stockings are seized, — Babel begun!

What a scene around the old hearth!
  What clattering words of delight!
'T would seem all the treasures of earth
  Were poured down the chimney last night.

"Oh, see what I 've got in my stocking!" —
  "Look here! and look here! and look here!"
The little groups round and round flocking,
  "Hope Christmas will last all the year."

They strew on the carpet their treasure, —
  Things useful, things pretty, things droll,
From Bibles they prize with such pleasure,
  To the little one's Lilliput doll.

They question how Santa Claus knows
  What each one has wished for so well,
And if in each house where he goes
  He every child's wishes can tell.

And where he gets all the good things,
  And how he can carry them all
In one little sled, when he brings
  Such lots to great children and small.

And how he can ride round the earth
  With his gifts in one single night,
And stop at each chimney and hearth,
  And always get through before light.

And why he has never been seen
  When driving his team through the air,
Nor when down the chimneys he 's been
  To leave all his gifts everywhere.

There 's one little urchin looks wise,
  And seems about bursting to tell
A thing that would open their eyes,
  And break the sweet Santa Claus' spell.

But thanks! the quick rattle and noise
  Rush timely to rescue the charm,
And save half the holiday joys
  From fatal and fast-coming harm.

Their child-joys will not pass away,
  But, locked in their hearts, will remain
To talk with them day after day,
  Till Christmas comes smiling again: —

To follow their pilgrimage far,
  To refill their hearts with delight,
And lead them along, like the star
  Which guided the wise men at night: —

Which guided their feet to the place
  Where the infant Redeemer they found,
And worshipped before his sweet face,
  And poured out their gifts on the ground.

CHRISTMAS-DAY.

Thus the merry Christmas-day
Passes rapidly away, —
Swiftly as an eagle's wing,
As they play and laugh and sing,
Now around the sparkling hearth,
Now upon the snow-clad earth.
  Snow and sled and skate and ice
Make a Winter-paradise.
Oh, the hours glide swiftly by
With such wings to help them fly!
  Yet not selfish pleasures bind
Generous children, heart and mind;
But they think of other's good,
Who have scantier fare and food;
But they think upon the poor,
Where few gifts go in the door;
And dividing theirs with such,
Make what 's left worth twice as much.

THE POOR.

OH, that men would help the poor,
Where few gifts go in the door!
They have not a Christmas-day,
Though they live not far away;
Th' hearth is cold, the table scant;
Sickness, poverty, and want
Dwell there now and long have dwelt;
Where the snow-banks never melt,
Where the sunbeams will not shine,
There take Christmas bread and wine!
Ask not now if there were guilt;
Think of scanty fire and quilt,
Think of woman, gentle-born,
By the wolves of hunger torn,
As she fought them day by day,
For her children's sake alway;
For her husband, till her strength
Failed her in the fight at length;
Think of her sweet children there
Shivering in the wintry air,
Huddling close to scanty hearth,
On this day of Jesus' birth,
When their hearts should dance with mirth,
When their little lips should sing
With the joys which you might bring!

Think of that poor suffering man,
Weary, wasted, worn and wan,
Bearing his and others' woe,
Penitent for aught you know,
Whom that faithful, watching wife
Nurses with her ebbing life!
Think of Christ and haste away,
Bearing gifts this Christmas-day!

CHRISTMAS-NIGHT.

THUS the merry Christmas-day
Passes rapidly away,
While they laugh and sing and play, —
While they think upon the poor,
Casting sunshine in his door, —
While they play and laugh and sing
Till the evening comes, to bring
To their merry, laughing group
Bright-eyed cousins, merry troop;
With Uncle Tom and Cousin Puff,
Should the evening not be rough;
All the promises are fair, —
Doctor Tom will sure be there;
So will round-faced, jolly Puff,
Sure as sneezing follows snuff:
If they come look out for fun,
Sure as light comes with the sun!

THE DOCTOR.

THE doctor is a man whose face
Not always finds a welcome place, —
Not always when he shows his bill,
Though always when a man is ill!
But Doctor Tom was welcome here,
As bird to Summer, all the year;
Though stern and grave in outward part,
He was a very child in heart, —
A doctor of the olden time,
With face as homely as my rhyme.
Tom was old when he was young, —
Old in looks and way and tongue,
Old in gait, and old in head,
Old in all he did and said;
Old and rusty,
Stale and musty,
Were the books he read.
Had you seen him when a child, —
Seen his face sedate and mild,
While his brothers played and smiled,
Had you judged him by his looks,
As he fumbled quaint old books,
Big as himself, you would have said
Here 's an old man newly bred,
Or old man turned into a child,

With his thoughtful face so mild.
Though all knew it was n't so,
Yet to all he seemed as though
They saw a man as old 's the Pope,
Through an inverted telescope.
  Thus was the doctor when a child,
Old, sedate, and grave, and mild;
But when mature, in manhood's prime,
He younger grew with flight of time;
Thus noble men, the truly great,
Still keep their hearts in child-estate.
  He "doctored" thousands in his day,
But always in a quaint, odd way; —
His nauseous drugs and tinctures vile
He mixed with wit and jolly guile,
And patients gulped them with a smile!
His pills and powders he would call
Gunpowder and his rifle-ball; —
With these he shot with deadly aim, —
Diseases and not men his game:
Some doctors think them both the same.
By art occult and intuition
He saw the sick man's true condition.
He trusted much to poohs! and pishes!
And abstinence from favorite dishes.
Where one had thought vile stuff to quaff
He oft prescribed a hearty laugh.
He dosed his patients with fresh air,

And wrapped them in the sunshine fair;
He recommended bat and ball
To young and old, to great and small;
Gave iron in the form of quoit,
Applied with skill by hand adroit;
He sometimes frowned disease away,
By reasoning kept a pain at bay,
Laughed the lank patient out of bed
Who thought the next day to be dead;
And seemed to know, by sort of magic,
When to look jolly and when tragic;
When to withhold and when to give,
To let one die, or let him live.
If sternly he denied the pain
One would not dare to groan again,
Or vomit, ache, or e'en complain.
His quaint face drove away the fear,
And with it went the sickness drear, —
An old-timed Doctor, honest, good!
Who never made dead men his food,
Nor kept men sick to keep himself
Well lined with capons, puffs, and pelf!

VAN PUFF.

BUT lined with all such was his cousin,
  And jolly as jolly could be,
And as large as a quarter o' dozen
  Of good Doctor Thomas was he!

The doctor approved his example,
  And held him up, not to a few,
As the very best sort of a sample
  Of just what no doctor could do.

"That a man can do without physic
  Just look at good Cousin Van Puff,
Except a slight touch of the phthisic,
  He 's sound as a log, and as tough!"

It would have astonished the visions
  Of a half score of sailors, or so,
To 've seen what a lot of provisions
  Van Puff daily stowed in below.

As if through two auger-holes peeping,
  Bored clean through two inches of meat,
His two little eyes, when not sleeping,
  Seemed looking for something to eat.

His round cheeks were always a-mating,
  And trying to meet, it was seen;
They, slowly, were thus suffocating
  The small nose that would stay between.

Though his heart seemed a mouse in a mountain,
  A large one, and merry enough,
Of kindly good feeling a fountain,
  Was the heart of good Cousin Van Puff.

THE SLEIGH-BELLS.

Hark! the merry sleigh-bells tingle
  On the listening ear: —
Or, is it other sounds that mingle
  With the wind we hear?

One runs quickly in and tells,
He has heard the coming bells!
Thinks it was the distant jingling
    Of the merry bells, —
And the evening winds were mingling
    With the bells!

Soon they 're watching, waiting, listening,
    At the open door,

Where the moon-lit snow is glistening
Like a diamond floor;
For the moon, in robes of light,
Dances on the snow to-night,
At the door.

Hark! the merry bells they hear!
Now more distant, now more near;
And nearer, nearer, —
The sounds grow clearer,
With their coming dingle-dingle,
And their jingling jingle-jingle,
And their mingling jingle-dingle,
Now faint and hardly heard,
Like notes of distant bird, —
Fainter, — still more faint they fall; —
Tinkling, then not heard at all, —
Are the bells.

Now again they rise and tingle
On the waiting ear,
And their dingle-dingle-dingle
You can plainly hear;
For they dingle near and nearer,
For they jingle clear and clearer,
With a merry dingle-dingle,
And a jolly jingle-jingle,
Coming near.

Again the sounds fall lower, —
The driver 's driving slower;
    They 're rising slowly up the hill,
    And the ringing tongues are still,
Save a faint-like tingle-tingle
With which evening, soft winds mingle, —
    With the bells.

They 've reached the summit, — dingle!
  What a rapid ringing dingling!
And the merry voices mingle
  With the dingle-dingling-jingling
    Of the bells.
  And each the other tells
  That he knows the merry bells, —
Knows the merry voices mingling
  With the jingling of the bells; —
    As they dingle,
    As they jingle,
With a trotting sort of dingle,
With a gallop of a jingle,
    Coming near and nearer;
    Ringing clear and clearer;
Till, with a jerk of a jingle,
    They halt at the gate,
And all the voices mingle
With that jerking jingle,
    At the gate!

THE ARRIVAL.

A SHAGGY bear and buffalo
Leap from the sleigh into the snow ; —
'T is Uncle Tom and Cousin Puff,
Wrapped in winter skin-robes rough.
Then little cousins bright and merry,
With cheeks as red as winter-berry,
And lips the same. Loose, tangled curls
Half hide the faces of the girls ; —
Who would not like to kiss such cousins,
Though they should come to him in dozens ?
So each one kisses rosy cousin,
Who "rather guess their toes are frozen,
And they themselves are numb almost ! "
But not their tongues are touched by frost ; —
Each one of these seems half a dozen, —
Each rattling tongue of female cousin ;
While midst the buffaloes and noise,
Two little, wrapped-up, red-cheeked boys,
Who look like grandsons of Jack Frost,
Are wellnigh in the hubbub lost.
At length they tumble from the straw,
And soon are taken where they 'll thaw ;
The glowing hearthstone smiles on them
Like sunlight on a ruddy gem.

THAWING.

Soon the bear and buffalo
  Shed their winter coats,
Soon the noisy tongues subside
  Into softer notes.

Soon a circle round the fire,
  'Neath the evergreen,
After health and friends inquire ;—
  Happier ne'er was seen!

Soon there bursts from Cousin Puff,
  While the talk goes on,
Laughter loud, but not too rough,
  Like a peal of fun: —

As a little youngster draws
  Close, with question tough,
"Say, are you good Santa Claus,
  Or only Cousin Puff?"

Twinkling with the merry thought,
  Puff first cons awhile
What good Christmas gifts he 's brought,
  The evening to beguile,

Whispers then in urchin's ear, —
  Imitating well, —
"Yes, I 'm Santa Claus, my dear,
  But you must not tell!

"Yes; I 'm Cousin Santa Claus,
  But it hurts my fat,
Squeezing through the chimney-flues,
  So I don't do that.

"But I come through open doors,
  When they 're not too small,
Where the jolly chimney roars,
  With good cheer for all."

Easily his plan was laid,
  For by all the laws,
Puff so jocund, rotund made,
  Looked like Santa Claus.

All at once he is unseen;
  But he 'll come back soon,
Dress'd all out in Christmas-green,
  Piping Christmas tune.

Children loved the genial face
  Glowing on Van Puff, —
Loved to join him in a race
  Up a high hill, rough,

Just to hear him laugh and blow
When the race was won,
And they all had beat him so,
Though he tried to run.

Fond of all the children throng
Was good Cousin Puff,
For he used to sing this song,
Looking very gruff: —

THE SONG OF SANTA CLAUS, V. P.

The man who would wantonly hurt a child,
Or break up its innocent play,
Should, if the penalty be not too mild,
Be banished to Botany Bay!

He 'd crush mother-birds in their downy nests,
Or shoot down their mates while they sing,
He 'd make a meal of young robin-redbreasts,
Or a broil of a pure cherub's wing.

Let no one trust him! his heart and his hand
And his tongue were made of old files;
Such a man, though born in a Christian land,
Got his soul from the Cannibal Isles.

SANTA CLAUS, V. P.

Hark! what a shout!
"Here 's Santa Claus! now boys, look out!
He never came here so before!
His reindeer team must be foot-sore,
Or else he 's driven the poor things dead,
Or else has broken down his sled!"
Such ringing, mingling screams and cheers
Hail Santa Claus when he appears
Arrayed so strangely to their sight,
In Christmas-greens and berries bright,
With beard so white, and long, and full,
It looked like rolls of carded wool;
Fantastic dress, and carrying pack
Of painted toys upon his back;
With pockets crammed with candies, cakes,
And all good things that Christmas bakes,
And picture-books more prized than pelf,
And many a doll, like fairy elf, —
Of colors red, and white, and dark, —
And all the beasts in Noah's ark,
And Noah's ark itself,
With Noah looking out!
Hark! what a shout!
What revel rout!
What ringing, mingling screams and cheers

Hail Santa Claus when he appears!
They grasp his hands and knees and pack,
They pull him down, climb on his back,
Each urchin, changed into an elf,
Cries, "Here is Santa Claus himself!
Come on, boys! let us hold him here,
And we 'll have Christmas all the year!"
He, pinned and hampered by the boys,
Disgorges pockets-full of toys,
And throws them from him, here and there,
To draw the urchins from his hair.
But back they come to pull and maul
Till they have got the treasures all,
And Cousin Santa Claus Van Puff,
Half-smothered, cries "Enough! enough!!"
And the old hearth laughs and sings,
And the old house cracks and rings,
Long after Cousin Puff
Has cried Enough!
They compromise to let him go,
But first demanding all to know,—
The girls more curious than the boys,—
Where Santa Claus gets all his toys.
Thus bound to tell, he, answering, said,
"Just as the wheat-fields bring forth bread,
Just as the spider weaves his web,
So from himself old Santa Claus
Brings out his gifts, by occult laws,

He 's full of cakes and dolls and toys, —
All sorts of gifts for girls and boys,
Which, when he 'd leave in happy home,
He moves a spring and out they come!
Fast as he gives them others grow;
That much about the saint we know; —
The more he gets the more he gives,
And that 's the way the good saint lives;
The more he gives the more he has,
Each year grows richer than he was,
And still keeps giving more and more,
And growing richer than before.
His cheeks grow rosier, and his girth
Grows larger, with good-will and mirth,
From Christmas-day to Christmas-day,
And, I suppose, will grow alway:
That 's all I know about the laws
And nature of good Santa Claus.
About his sled and tiny deer,
And where he keeps them all the year,
And how he goes from house to house,
As sly and softly as a mouse,
And gets down chimney with a pack
As big as I am on his back,
And drives his reindeer through the air,
Why, ask him when you see him there!"

THE FEAST.

WHILE yet he spake a savory smell,
  Like courier of the coming feast,
Came to good Santa Claus to tell
  What he was ready for at least.

For Santa Claus was never one
  From festive board to turn his heel,
And never was so full of fun
  He could not hold a hearty meal.

The ample board, with dainties spread,
  Is doubly blest with prayer and praise
To Him who gives us daily bread,
  And merry hearts, and festive days.

And glad and full the feast they share,
  But heed the cautious word divine,
Not make the table evil snare,
  Nor tarry at the tempting wine.

GAMES.

TIME flies; and yet the merry Christmas flame
Must smile, before they part, on many a game,
But chief among them all, though sometimes rough,

The best and merriest, good old Blind-Man's-
Buff!
For this they stormed the kitchen's ample
space, —
The kitchen famous for its fireplace, —
Of breadth four feet, in length full half a score,
Where old birch-logs so loved to blaze and roar
And send their beams across the oaken floor,
Here Pete and Till, an Ethiop king and
queen,
Their kingdom kept, and kept their kingdom
clean.
No longer slaves, they loved the Homestead
still, —
Pete left it afterwards, but never Till.
Here parents, children, servants, great and
small,
Now join the sport, nor heed the bruise or
fall.

BLIND-MAN'S-BUFF.

BIND the bandage tight and fairly,
Trip away, then, light and warily!
Beware! take care!
Sport is sport when not too rough;
Take care! beware!
Playing Blind-Man's-Buff.

"Now I 'll have you, here or there,
By the coat, or dress, or hair!"
        Feeling, fumbling,
        Reeling, stumbling,
"Now I 've got you!" grasps the air.
While the merry laugh rings out,
Mingling with the louder shout,
And the din grows loud enough,
        Playing Blind-Man's-Buff.

Guided by the noise, he reaches
Quick the place of shouts and screeches; —
        How they scatter!
        Calling, guiding,
        Falling, hiding;
        Small feet patter,
        Loud tongues clatter,
Then a stillness still as death;
Every one must hold his breath,
Though he needs to pant and puff,
        Playing Blind-Man's-Buff!

Now a stifled laugh leaps out,
Near the shuffling Blind-man's route,
        From under a table; —
        Quick as thought
        The wretch is caught!
        And a perfect Babel
        Of wild uproar

Shakes the ceiling and oaken floor!
The tables are turning,
The Blind-man 's blind no more;
Each one as happy as he
Hurras for his victory!
Rapping, thumping,
Clapping, jumping;
The old fire does his part
In his place,
Crackling and burning,
Dull care spurning;
He glows with a ruddier face,
He throws his arms about;
And all are merry, though few are free
From a fit of Blind-man's gout,
For who escapes a fall or cuff,
Playing Blind-Man's-Buff?

Now the victim caught, blindfolded,
Laughed at, pinched and pushed and scolded,
Must take his turn;
And so the game
Goes round the same;
And bright fires burn
In every heart and dance in every eye,
And paint the healthy cheek with rosy dye;
And every limb grows stronger,
And every life grows longer,

The heart more free, the body tough,
Playing Blind-Man's-Buff!

FLOWERS AND GEMS OF THE OLDEN TIME.

THUS Christmas passed in olden time,
In the sweet vale where we have stood,
Not dreaming aught of care or crime,
But only of the pure and good.

Our fathers' faults, whate'er they were,
We throw a mantle over them;
Only their virtues we transfer,
More worth than kingly diadem.

We go not to the buried Past,
To call to life its evil men,
We go not to our fathers' graves
To bid their dead faults live again;

We go to gather flowers there, —
Sweet flowers on good men's graves are found, —
We go to bring back jewels rare, —
Gems hid too long beneath the ground.

In our own gardens we would grow
  These flowers of a better clime,
In our own bosoms we would show
  These jewels of the olden time.

In our own Homesteads we would light
  The fires that made theirs what they were, —
The dearest spots to human sight,
  And beacons to the wanderer.

Their frugal fare gave jocund health, —
  Elixir of perennial bloom ;
Their labor gave them more than wealth, —
  Plenty, without the rich man's doom.

Their simple sports gave manly strength,
  Which broke stern Winter's icy crown,
For Winter always smiles, at length,
  On them who bravely meet his frown :

And growing sportive, even seeks
  To catch the shrinking damsel fair,
And roses blush upon the cheeks,
  He kisses in the open air.

NOW AND THEN.

Since then what rapid changes men have
made! —
With restless energy of pick and spade
What valleys they have filled, what mountains
riven,
For Satan's iron track to vex high heaven!

Beelzebub has drawn his sulphurous train;
And driven the wedge to split the land in
twain;
And on our shores, from o'er the seas, has
hurled
The vile corruptions of a worn-out world.

Our honest fathers would have burned with
rage
To see the fruits of our degenerate age, —
To see the land o'ergrown with vicious weeds,
Where, in our day, the devil has sown his seeds.

Indulgent parents toil till they are old
To pave their children's path of life with gold, —
The shining path their darling offspring take,
By easy grades, down to the burning lake!

How pleased the eye to turn from scenes like
this
To those old times of simple, rural bliss!
We lingering turn, though forced to pass along,
To catch once more the mirth and joyous
song; —

To greet once more the old Homestead's ruddy
face,
Beaming glad welcome to his warm embrace; —
To see the light of Summer in his smiles,
Which wintry night and heavy care beguiles.

His glowing heart, his genial face a-blaze,
Make winter evenings pass like summer-days,
And make sweet roses bloom all winter long
Upon the faces of the household throng.

Their faces shine, — we hear their merry
tongue,
But hear no sobs about the truant young!
The truant young from cheerless homesteads
come,
And children, in those times, found joys at
home:

These bound them by a thousand sacred ties,
Which made the home a doorway to the skies;

And symbol of the House prepared above
For human hearts that burn with holy love.

And perfume sweeter than a summer rose
Spreads through the Homestead, at the evening's close,
From prayer's sweet incense, and the odorous sweep
Of angels' wings, who guard them while they sleep.

THE PARTING.

But list! they gather for the parting song, —
The evening hours have borne them far along,
And some must ride, — their teams are at the gate, —
And tinkling sleigh-bells now impatient wait.

So gathering round they come, though loth to part,
Expressing each to each their thankful heart
For evening's joy; and while the fire burns bright,
They sing to Him whose throne is love and light; —

They sing to Him whose humble human birth
Gave life and breath and song to Christmas
mirth;
Who, conquering Death, robbed Death itself
of gloom,
And filled the grave with light and sweet per-
fume.

To Him they sing who gives the Homestead-
cheer;
And love's sweet, sacred ties, than life more
dear,
Which freights with joy each passing word that
flies,
And makes it drop a blessing ere it dies.

To Him they sing who lights the Christian
hearth;
Who brought the songs of angels to the earth;
Who kindles in the heart a heavenly fire,
Whose burning flames to heaven itself aspire;

Who was in swaddling clothes in manger laid,
That they might be in robes of light arrayed;
And houseless went that He might build for
them
A Homestead in the New Jerusalem.

THE CHRISTMAS-SONG.

Christ now wears His crown of glory,
  But He left His manger here, —
Left with us His humble story, —
  Every lowly heart to cheer.

Christ, the Lord, was born of woman,
  Oh the kind, mysterious plan!
Christ, because His heart is human,
  Knows the feelings of a man.

Christ was laid within a manger,
  On the night that He was born,
That the poor and houseless stranger
  Might take heart on Christmas morn.

Christ Himself was weak and weary
  With the load his Father gave,
Sorrowful His pathway dreary
  Led Him onward to the grave.

But He bore the load for others, —
  Poverty and pain and loss,
All for us, His younger brothers,
  From the manger to the cross.

Christ good gifts to men has given
  Ever since His blessed birth;
Flowers and fruits that grow in heaven
  Are His footprints on the earth.

Bear abroad the gladdening sources
  Of the joy which we have found!
Like the sunlight in its courses
  Let the Christmas cheer go round!

Bear the bread and wine of heaven
  To the hungry and forlorn,
Which to feed the poor was given
  When the Holy Child was born.

With the angels keep on singing
  Of the blessed Saviour's birth,
Till the song be ever ringing
  In a chorus round the earth:

Till it quench the fires of malice
  Burning in the human blood,
Till it light in hut and palace
  Fires of love to men and God.

Till the prison-doors fly open,
  And the sightless eyeballs see,
When the dungeons that they grope in
  Are exchanged for liberty:

Till it strengthen all who falter,
  Till it guide the erring right,
As it makes each home and altar
  To resound with heaven's delight.

Sing it till from stream and fountain,
  Flowing river, boisterous main,
Hill-side, field, and skyward mountain,
  Earth shall join the angel strain, —

Singing of the wondrous story, —
  Of the blessed Saviour's birth, —
Glory in the highest! glory
  Be to God! and peace on earth!

GOOD-NIGHT!

I 'LL never forget that parting song,
  Nor the echoing notes of delight
Which bore it, like angel chorus, along
  Through the Christmas air that night!

I 'll never forget the dear, old Hearth
  Which made the old Homestead so bright;
I 'll never forget its joy and mirth,
  Nor its merry, old Christmas light.

I 'll never forget the faces there,
  Which shine now, like stars, in the skies;
And though I may see others more fair,
  They never seem so in my eyes.

I 'll never forget the voices which sang,
  With a sacred joy and a might,
Till the dear old Homestead walls, all rang,
  When the music was at its height.

I 'll never forget the grasp of the hand,
  Nor the dear friends who said, — "Good-Night!"
Till I meet them in the Brighter Land,
  In a ceaseless round of delight.

THE END.

www.ingramcontent.com/pod-product-compliance
Lightning Source LLC
LaVergne TN
LVHW011119110826
845150LV00008B/2186

* 9 7 8 1 4 2 5 5 0 6 8 1 0 *